STEVEN VAN HOLLAND

Lekker Direct

Surviving the Netherlands One Awkward Moment at a Time - Black & White Edition

Contents

1

Introduction - The Ugly Truth

One might think the ugly truth is a mythical beast, like Bigfoot in the US or the Loch Ness Monster in Scotland — lurking in dark alleys, peeking around corners, mostly hidden.

Not in The Netherlands, dear readers.

Here, the ugly truth strolls in broad daylight, mingling freely among crowds — crowds that may well include your family and closest friends. No need for blurry photos or conspiracy theories; it's right there. Walk around for a bit, and I promise — you'll meet it.

But don't worry. Amid the bold directness, awkward remarks, and seemingly hurtful comments, there's a surprising kind of friendliness and respect that might just win you over.

This book explores Dutch culture — not academically, not with a pros-and-cons list — but through the eyes of a foreigner. Together, we'll uncover the awkward, funny, and downright bizarre situations that expats (and brave visitors) in The Netherlands can expect to stumble into.

Though written from a foreigner's perspective, this book is for Dutch readers too — and anyone curious about cultural quirks. Many of these insights only exist because I've lived elsewhere, and because so many wonderful international friends have shared their worlds with me.

So grab a coffee, add a stroopwafel, and join me. Through bicycle-filled streets, unspoken (and loudly spoken) rules, and those infamous three kisses on the cheek, we'll laugh, cringe, and discover together. It's going to be an adventure — or, for some, maybe a flashback.

2

Welcome to The Netherlands, what do you want?

What do you want?

Pablo and Isabella, a vibrant Spanish couple, had just landed in Amsterdam.

Isabella had found a new job that brought them to the Low Countries, and Pablo worked remotely — ready to follow wherever adventure took them.

Armed with their optimism (and a translation app), they set out to explore the charming streets of their new home.

First Encounter with Dutch Directness

Their first brush with "The Direct Dutch" came faster than expected.

While looking for their hotel, they asked a passerby for directions.

The woman, friendly but straightforward, immediately rattled off:

> "Oh, it's just a ten-minute walk from here. But don't take that street, it's a bit longer. Go left, right, left again, cross two bridges, then turn right. Easy peasy!"

Before Pablo and Isabella could even ask for clarification, she smiled, hopped on her bike, and zipped away.

> Pablo blinked.
> "Did you catch all of that?" he asked Isabella with a half-laugh.
> Isabella shook her head, equally bewildered but determined.
> "We'll find it… somehow."

A Café Conversation

Later that afternoon, they stopped at a cozy café to regroup.

Isabella, eager to dive into Dutch food culture, asked the barista:

> "What's the best Dutch pastry?"

Without missing a beat, the barista replied matter-of-factly:

"Most tourists order stroopwafels. Try that."

"We're actually not tourists," Isabella explained, "we're relocating here."

The barista nodded politely, unimpressed.

"Would you like milk and sugar with your coffee?"

It wasn't even busy in the café. Pablo and Isabella exchanged a glance — was the barista just having a bad day?

When settling the bill, Pablo tried another friendly approach.

"Those stroopwafels were delicious. This must be the best place in town for them!"

The barista laughed out loud.

"Haha! Not even close. Try the ones they make at the market. Ours are nothing — theirs are huge! You can top them with chocolate, more caramel, whipped cream, even butter. Go before lunch, or you'll need a nap after."

Before they could respond, she waved them off cheerily.

Walking out, Pablo whispered:

"Well... no beating around the bush here."

At the Museum

A few days later, they joined a group tour at a museum.

When the guide asked where everyone was from, Pablo proudly announced:

"¡Somos de España!" ("We are from Spain!")

The guide smiled, nodded… and immediately moved on to the next topic without asking a single question.

Pablo leaned over to Isabella and grinned:

"I guess nobody's interested in our life story here!"

A More Personal Misunderstanding

Isabella's biggest cultural shock came at work.

One afternoon, she invited her colleague Tom to join a meeting scheduled for the next day.

Tom declined politely, explaining:

"I won't be coming in. My grandfather passed away. The funeral is tomorrow."

Isabella's eyes widened. She hesitated, then softly said:

"Het spijt me." *("I'm sorry.")*

Tom smiled gently, patting her on the shoulder:

"Oh, not needed. You didn't know."

As he turned away, Isabella noticed a flicker of sadness in his eyes — and felt a pang of confusion.

Linda, another colleague sitting nearby, leaned in and whispered:

"We don't usually apologize for things we didn't cause.

Tom thinks you're apologizing for asking him to join the meeting — not about his grandfather."

Isabella's cheeks flushed red.

"Oh my."

"No worries," Linda reassured her.

> "Just say 'gecondoleerd' next time — it's the Dutch way."

Welcome to The Netherlands

And so, Pablo and Isabella began their life in the Netherlands.

While they struggled at first to fully grasp Dutch directness — especially the complete lack of subtle emotional signals —

they quickly learned to appreciate the honesty, the clarity, and the quirky charm hidden behind it all.

> *(Even in Dutch bluntness, subtlety exists... but you have to know where to look. Luckily for us, Pablo and Isabella aren't done bumping into it just yet. Their story continues in Chapter 6: Kingsday)*

3

Scheduling all social events

Maar schoonmoeder wat doet u buiten in de regen en de kou. Ga maar snel naar huis voordat u ziek wordt! "But mother in law what are you doing standing outside in the rain and cold weather. Go home quickly before you become ill!"

Whilst the above example might be both a joke and an exaggeration, Dutch people in general do not participate in spontaneous visits from friends or family. With some friends or family members that you are in constant contact with, you might just pop in — but that is only because you know their schedule. You know they are at home, just slouching around.

Making an appointment to visit friends or family

The reason why the Dutch don't often go for a spontaneous visit and prefer to plan is twofold. First of all, it comes from a very logical thinking process focused on time and efficiency (this will come back a lot in this book). With a spontaneous visit, simply said, you do not know what they have planned — you might arrive just as they have to leave in 10 minutes. You don't even know if they are home, so it might result in you wasting your time.

Secondly, although the Dutch love socializing — especially on a terrace while wearing ugly sunglasses — they value their personal space. A moment they did not plan to socialize, even if they are technically available, is considered invasive. After all, it is a small effort to quickly WhatsApp (or dare I say call?) them to ask about their plans.

An Illustrative Story

Let's take Dimitrios and Eleni. They are both Greek natives who decided to relocate to The Netherlands. One sunny afternoon, Dimitrios and Eleni were feeling adventurous and wanted to surprise their Dutch friends, Hans and Marijke. Hans and Marijke had just settled into their new home, only a few blocks away from our Greek friends.

Excitedly, Dimitrios and Eleni put on their walking shoes and embarked on their spontaneous visit. Little did they know that the Dutch had a different approach to unexpected guests.

As they arrived at Hans and Marijke's doorstep, Dimitrios exclaimed, "Eleni, let's knock on the door and surprise them with our homemade Koulouri."

Eleni nodded, equally enthusiastic. They knocked on the door, and after a few moments, Marijke opened it with a surprised expression on her face.

> "Oh, Dimitrios and Eleni, how nice to see you. Hans didn't tell me you were coming," she said, grinding her teeth slightly and shooting Hans a look.
>
> "Oh, we didn't tell him," they exclaimed. "We just decided to come over this morning!"

"Ah, that explains it," she responded, her voice lightening a bit.

"Feel free to come in for a moment, but I have to leave in 10 minutes. I promised to bring my mother groceries at 14:00 — and it's five before half two already," she added quickly. *(That, dear reader, is 13:25 in normal human language.)*

Dimitrios and Eleni exchanged confused glances. No words were spoken, but the confusion was clear. Before they could respond, Marijke continued briskly:

"Look, why don't we meet next Sunday instead? If you are available at the same time, I'll just tell my mother I'll be there at 16:00 next week. Or wait… I believe Jan doesn't have his regular club meeting next Saturday. What about then?"

Dimitrios and Eleni left, a little disappointed and very confused.

"Do they not like us?" Eleni whispered to Dimitrios.

"They invited us for Sunday… but maybe they meant another Sunday? Is that a thing here?"

Dimitrios shrugged. "I guess we'll find out."

Whilst social life in Greece has a totally different approach, over time they actually ended up obliging (or should I say succumbing?) to the Dutch way. And although they would never admit this to their family, as time went on and their social calendar filled up with pre-planned dinners and coffees, they began to see the appeal of knowing exactly when — and with whom — their time would be spent. They even came to appreciate the benefits of a little more personal space.

Still, every once in a while, when someone mentions an "impromptu coffee," Dimitrios and Eleni can't help but chuckle — and think back to the afternoon they learned that even spontaneity has a schedule in The Netherlands.

<h1 style="text-align:center">4</h1>

Only 'No' means 'No'

Hinting at 'No' is a real challenge if not impossible

Coming over for a coffee

Nigel had been invited to his Dutch colleague Hans's house for coffee — a simple affair, he'd been told.

A bit of gezelligheid.

What Nigel hadn't realized was that "simple" in the Netherlands could indeed include cake.

"Appeltaart," Hans announced proudly, setting down a plate of what could only be described as a golden, cinnamon-laden, slightly overcooked result of Hans's best efforts.

Nigel took a cautious bite, immediately overwhelmed by a combination of dry pastry and an overzealous use of cinnamon.

"Oh, it's…" He paused, searching desperately for a word that wouldn't betray his true feelings.

"Rustic."

Hans beamed.

"Thank you! It's my first time making one. My mother said, 'Hans, stick to the bakery,' but I thought, why not try? So, you like it?"

Nigel swallowed hard.

"It's, um, bold. A very bold interpretation."

"Have another piece!" Hans said proudly, reaching for the knife.

Nigel's stomach dropped.

"Oh, no, really, I couldn't possibly. One slice was more than enough. A real… treat."

Hans paused mid-slice.

"You couldn't?"

"No, no, really, it was delightful," Nigel insisted hurriedly, trying to sound effusive while desperately signaling 'no more, please.'

"I'd hate to deprive someone else of the joy."

Hans glanced around the empty room.

"Who would you be depriving?"

Nigel hesitated.

"Well, uh, you. Or perhaps… future guests?"

Hans frowned slightly.

"Future guests? Too bad for them, right? I didn't invite anyone else."

Nigel squirmed.

"Well, it's just… I'm trying to be good, you know. Doctor's orders. A bit of moderation."

"Moderation?" Hans repeated, sounding out the word like it was a foreign concept.

"Exactly! Moderation," Nigel said, nodding earnestly.

Hans placed the freshly cut slice on a plate and set it down in front of Nigel.

"I have moderated it to two pieces now."

Nigel stared at the plate, aghast.

"Well, that's… one way of looking at it, I suppose."

He leaned back, raising his hands politely.

"Honestly, Hans, I'm quite full. I'd hate to deprive you of it. You made it yourself—you should enjoy it!"

Hans looked genuinely puzzled.

"But I made it for us. Why would I deprive myself?"

"Well, yes, but I insist—"

Hans interrupted, setting down the second slice with finality.

"Nigel, you insist too much. In the Netherlands, if you don't want something, you just say no. Not 'I couldn't,' not 'I shouldn't,' not 'I'd hate to.' Just: no."

Hans leaned back, his expression kind but firm.

"Simple. No."
   "I did say no," Nigel protested weakly.

Hans shook his head.

"No. You said, 'I couldn't possibly,' and something about future guests."

Nigel blinked, horrified by the brutal simplicity of Hans's logic.

"But that's terribly... direct."

"Exactly," Hans said, nodding gravely. "We're Dutch. Now... eet smakelijk."

Nigel sighed, defeated, and picked up his fork.

"Well, when in Rome... or, uh, Rotterdam..." he muttered, steeling himself for round two of culinary endurance.

The pie, if possible, was even worse the second time around.

As Hans poured another enthusiastic round of coffee — strong enough to revive a corpse — Nigel made a mental note for next time:

Bring biscuits. And a rock-solid excuse.

5

To Queue or Not To Queue — That is the (Dutch) Question

A new till just opened

The Checkout Grand Prix

Marcus, a polite British expat, prided himself on his impeccable queueing skills.

Neat, orderly, respectful — the true pillars of any civilized society.

Or so he thought.

Until he faced the Dutch supermarket.

It started innocently enough: a long, patient line at the checkout, quiet murmurs, the soft clink of shopping carts.

Marcus clutched his basket, content to wait his turn in dignified British silence.

Then, without warning — *DING!* — a cashier flipped on the light at a newly opened till.

The atmosphere changed instantly.

Pensioners with baskets surged forward like sprinters at the Olympics.

Teenagers launched tactical strikes from the candy aisle.

A woman with a double stroller executed a hairpin turn worthy of Monaco.

A pensioner rammed into a display of *pindakaas*, sending chemicals into the battlefield air — luckily nobody with a peanut allergy was nearby.

Marcus stood frozen, his loaf of bread clutched like a shield.

By the time he blinked, the new till was already packed — his dream of swift checkout crushed under a stampede of determined Dutch shoppers.

> "Good heavens," he muttered. "It's not a queue… it's a Grand Prix with groceries."

Learning the Hard Way

That evening, Marcus sat on his sofa, analyzing his performance like a defeated race engineer.

His strategy had been sound — but his reflexes? Hopelessly British.

If he was to survive Dutch supermarket culture, he would need to adapt.

Study the enemy. Train.

Become the racer.

He made a silent vow:

> "Next time… no prisoners."

Race Day

One week later, armed with newfound determination and wearing his best sneakers ("lightweight, for agility"), Marcus returned to the battlefield.

He positioned himself carefully in the supermarket layout: not too close to the tills, not too deep into the bakery section where temptation could slow him down.

Muscles tense.

Eyes locked onto the cashier area with laser precision.

Then — *DING!* — a new till opened.

GO!

Marcus launched forward like a McLaren off the starting grid.

A pensioner tried to cut him off with a basket full of *hagelslag* and cleaning spray — Marcus slipstreamed neatly behind a woman pushing a suspiciously empty cart, using her as moving cover.

He dodged a toddler wielding a rogue baguette like a lightsaber.

He veered left, narrowly missing a fallen box of *hagelslag* — chocolatey debris scattered across the aisle like an oil slick.

"Yellow flag conditions," he thought grimly, adjusting his racing line.

A woman attempted a cheeky block with her cart — Marcus pulled a Verstappen, diving down the inside line with steely resolve.

A near-disaster struck when a kid threw a bottle of Fristi across the aisle like a Molotov cocktail.

Marcus hopped over it like a man possessed.

The finish line — the blessed new till — was in sight.

With a final burst of speed (and perhaps a small tactical hip-check that surely fell within supermarket ethics), Marcus slid into position: third in line.

Podium finish! He fought the urge to punch the air in victory — barely.

Reflection

As he placed his groceries proudly on the conveyor belt —

a loaf of bread, a box of *hagelslag* (battle-scarred but intact), and a suspiciously dented bottle of mayonnaise — Marcus grinned.

"Max Verstappen, eat your heart out," he whispered to himself.

He had conquered the chaos.

He had survived the thrown obstacles.

He had outrun rogue baguette-wielding toddlers.

Victory was sweet. Sweeter than *hagelslag.*

Sweeter even than getting exact change on the first try.

As he pushed his cart toward the parking lot under the grey Dutch sky, he allowed himself a final, satisfied thought:

> "Surviving the Dutch supermarket?
>   One small step toward truly understanding Dutch culture…
>   and one giant leap for expat-kind."

If only he would have remembered his 'bonus card'…

6

Kingsday

Kingsday

Pablo and Isabella, a spirited Spanish couple, had recently embarked on their Dutch adventure. Relocating to the Netherlands

They had marveled at the canals, survived their first cycling attempts, and even managed to say *fiets* without giggling.

But nothing — absolutely nothing — had prepared them for Kingsday.

The Madness Begins

Pablo and Isabella, blissfully unaware of Kingsday or what it entailed, were simply out for a walk.

They ran into a beaming Dutch student holding a half-deflated orange balloon in one hand and a can of spray paint in the other.

> "Those are the wrong shirts," he said, staring at the second-hand
> football jerseys they'd proudly scored the day before — crisp white,
> bold black stripes, and a suspiciously German eagle.
> "We got them for one euro each," Pablo offered. "Vintage!"

The student didn't blink. He casually pulled an orange spray can from his
backpack and gave it a vigorous shake.

Pssshht.

Before they realized what had happened, a fine coat of orange mist graced
their shoulders.

> "What is this? Assault?" Pablo stuttered

The student calmly handed them each a wrinkled T-shirt from his backpack
— one reading *"De Oranje Leeuw"*, the other *"88."*

> "Put these on. Trust me. You'll be happier."

Then he vanished, balloon dragging behind him like a popped parachute.
Pablo looked confused.

> "Well... do we trust the native assailant who gives out free T-shirts?"
> "I think we've been culturally corrected," Isabella said flatly.

Into the Chaos

The city center hit them like a confetti cannon.

Everything was orange: hats, scarves, shoes, sunglasses — even dogs in tiny
vests and someone's parrot in an orange tutu.

They wandered into a sprawling freemarket. Every family in town had
apparently emptied their attic onto blankets and foldable tables.

> "Pablo, look at this," Isabella whispered. "It's like a garage sale exploded onto the street."

They marveled at the randomness: stacks of used board games missing half the pieces, single shoes (*"buy one, good luck finding the other"*), and a warped vinyl of Julio Iglesias titled *Summer Heatwave '85* melting quietly in the sun.

A small child sprinted past them, clutching a bright helium balloon.

It immediately popped against a passing bicycle handle.

He burst into tears. The cyclist barely looked up and shouted some apparent profanities into the distance.

> 'Don't worry kiddo' Said Pablo 'here you can have this chocolate bar' 'lekker!' The kid took the chocolate and sprinted away

The Bitterbal Incident

Later, feeling brave (and mildly peckish), Pablo reached for a tray of steaming bitterballen near a food stand.

> "Careful," the vendor warned, "they're hot."

Pablo nodded — *I can handle spicy food,* he thought — and popped one in his mouth.

He instantly inhaled fire.

"AGHHmmhhot–" he managed, eyes watering, hopping in place like a man fighting invisible bees.

> Isabella tried not to laugh. Tried.
> "Spicy?" she asked.
> "Nooo-ho-ho-HOT," he wheezed, as tears streamed down his face and he fanned his mouth like a flamenco dancer in crisis.

He finally swallowed and wheezed:

> "I think I no longer have a tongue."
>
> "That would be very unfortunate," grinned Isabella with a small devilish smile.

The Juice That Wasn't

They continued their crawl through the celebration, eventually pausing near a group of teenagers huddled together around suspiciously colored bottles.

"Why do they all look like they're hiding soda from the police?" Pablo asked.

"Or conducting a very bad chemistry experiment," Isabella added.

One teen grinned and handed Pablo a plastic cup filled with what looked like orange Fanta.

He took a sip. Then blinked.

"This tastes like vodka, gummy bears, and regret."

A nearby woman overheard and raised her own bottle of glowing magenta liquid.

"To bad decisions and… whatever!" she cheered.

The Wig Incident

Just when they thought they'd seen it all, they spotted a man wearing an enormous orange wig, dancing with dangerous enthusiasm to an accordion player's frantic tune.

He spun. Wobbled. Spun again.

And then crashed headfirst into a lamppost with a dull *THUNK*.

The wig flew through the air like a startled flamingo… and landed with a graceful *plop* in the canal.

Pablo clutched his stomach laughing.

> "Is it still considered a dignified celebration if you have to fish your hair out of the water?"

The soggy dancer retrieved the wig with surprising calm, wrung it out like a wet sponge, and plopped it back on his head without missing a beat.

Isabella wiped tears from her eyes.

"This man is my hero."

Canal Reflections

As the sun dipped low and the last echoes of accordion music faded, Pablo and Isabella found a quiet spot by the canal.

The once-bustling streets now wore a tired, satisfied, and appropriately orange glow. A bicycle floated upside-down in the water. A lonely plastic cup drifted past like a forgotten boat.

"It's incredible how the whole country became a festival," Pablo said.

"From attic treasures to airborne wigs…" Isabella replied, adjusting her now lopsided Kingsday crown.

"I've cracked it. Kingsday is just St. Patrick's Day — but warmer, and orange."

Just as they prepared to leave, the balloon boy from earlier reappeared — this time holding a bright orange tulip.

"¡Para ustedes!" he beamed, proud as one can be.

Pablo accepted it with a gracious bow.

"Thank you, little king! Long may you reign."

As they wandered home — orange T-shirts crumpled, cheeks aching from laughter, tulip in hand — Pablo leaned toward Isabella and whispered:

"You know, *in Nederland gaat het er soms Spaans aan toe*." (*"In the Netherlands, it sometimes goes Spanish."*[*])

Isabella laughed, linking her arm through his.

"At least today, we fit right in."

(*) More on Dutch sayings and expressions — like "In Nederland gaat het er soms Spaans aan toe" — will be explored in a future book dedicated

entirely to the wonderful, weird, and wildly direct world of Dutch expressions. Stay tuned

7

Timekeeping Extremism

Dutch hospitality meets Italian expectations.

Dutch Are Timekeeping Extremists

In fact, Dutch people are so disgusted by tardiness that they would almost prefer to admit they appreciate Germans.

(*Reference: see chapter "Dutch Neighbours."*)

Everything is planned and scheduled: business meetings, the meeting of the local sport club, an appointment at the barber — believe it or not, even their social lives.

It is more common than not to schedule when to meet your best friend at the bar.

Also, agreeing to meet at 20:00 means you agree to meet at 20:00.

If they are over five minutes late, they will let the other person know, explain, and apologize.

Let's take a realistic scenario about how this can play out with two expats who are unfamiliar with this Dutch cultural aspect.

Scenario:

Meet Sofia and Antonio. An Italian couple who just moved to The Netherlands and are renting a house in a picturesque Dutch village near Groningen.

They are known for their passion for food and their love of long, indulgent social dinners.

One fateful evening, when the weather was actually nice for once in this northern part of The Netherlands, they received an invitation from their Dutch friends, Klaas and Linda from the next town over, for what our Italian friends imagined was going to be a delightful feast at Klaas and Linda's house.

Sofia and Antonio, being true Italians, arrived fashionably late — a whole hour and a half behind schedule.

They rang the doorbell with anticipation, expecting the sounds and scents of a sumptuous dinner party to greet them upon entry.

Klaas opened the door with a puzzled look on his face.

"Antonio! Sofia! You're here! What happened? Is everything okay with the two of you?" uttered Klaas with a confused and slightly worried expression.

"We are fine, what do you mean?" was Antonio's response.

"Well, dinner was at 18:00, and it's over 19:30 now," was Klaas's response.

His worried look reasonably quickly faded into only slight confusion before it moved into acceptance, and he shrugged his shoulders, saying,

"But come in."

Sofia, clearly the more aware of the two, was quick to realize the cultural difference and instantly apologized for the slightly awkward situation, sensing the confusion and light setback of their host.

Dutch food & hospitality

When walking into the living room, they were met by Linda and a lovely atmosphere with many dimmed lights and background music.

However, it was once again Sofia spotting the oddity.

"Oh how lovely how you decorated your living room, but where is the food if I might ask?" she exclaimed.

"Oh well, we had dinner and it has just been cleared away since you weren't expected to show up anymore," was Klaas's response.

"And to be honest, we gave the remainders to my brother who just left. He is going to share it with his boyfriend who is working late today."

Antonio's eyes widened in disbelief, and Sofia was internally fighting to stop her mouth from dropping open in dismay.

They had imagined a table brimming with culinary delights, but now they were left empty-handed.

Like the Dutch saying goes: *They found the dog in the pot!* (*Ze vonden de hond in de pot!*) (*)

Linda reassured them:

"Oh, don't worry! We still have some snacks left, and I'm sure we can whip up something for you. Let's salvage this situation, shall we?"

> *"Oh, that is not needed"* would have been a dire mistake, dear reader.
> This would not be considered polite, but by many Dutch people would be 'misunderstood' as "I literally do not want to eat."

Luckily, Antonio was aware of this trait of Dutch culture and instantly responded with,

"I appreciate that."

Sofia showed off her Dutch language skills:

"*Graag!*" was her response — which received a delayed smile and a chuckle when Klaas and Linda processed what Sofia was saying.

Just a few minutes later, Klaas returned with two microwaved soggy pizzas (of which one was Hawaiian), bought from the deep-freeze aisle (at a discount, of course) from Albert Heijn.

A microwaved and discounted masterpiece!

Proudly, he put the "food" in front of Sofia and Antonio.

As Antonio and Sofia consumed the calories, their initial disappointment transformed into laughter and amusement.

They joked about how their tardiness had caused such a comical turn of events.

According to both Antonio and Sofia, time in Italy — especially during social events — is not so important as it clearly is in The Netherlands.

When leaving, however, they made the mistake of saying the food was good, setting themselves up for future misery delivered at the hands of Dutch eating habits.

It was not all bad, though.

On December 5th, our Italians received a curious gift.

Wrapped neatly was a painting of a wall clock — a clock with no arms.

Attached to it was a short note that read:

> *"This is a fitting gift — for this Italian couple, time is only ecstatic."*

Antonio blinked at the painting, scratching his head.

"Is this Dutch art?" he asked, holding the picture sideways as if that might reveal hidden meaning.

Across the room, Sofia fought back a laugh as she noticed the small figure tucked into the background of the scene:

An old man in a red robe, carrying a staff, frowning sternly down from a painted window.

It seems the spirit of *Sinterklaas* was keeping an eye on them after all.

(Read more about this event in the chapter about "Sinterklaas.")

> *(*) More on Dutch sayings and expressions — like "Ze vonden de hond in de pot" — will be explored in a future book dedicated entirely to the wonderful, weird, and wildly direct world of Dutch expressions. Stay*

tuned

35

8

Rokjesdag Revelations: An American Woman Experiences 'Skirts Day'

Lars getting 'caught'

Rokjesdag Revelations

An American named Emily found herself in a destination she had never anticipated:

The Netherlands.

She had relocated for work in late autumn, and now, as spring approached, she heard whispers of a peculiar tradition known as *Rokjesdag*.

She overheard colleagues mentioning it and, intrigued, asked about it.

They told her it was a phenomenon — a celebration marking the unofficial arrival of spring.

With curiosity sparked, Emily set out to experience this uniquely Dutch rite of passage firsthand.

As winter's chill finally began to fade, Emily noticed a palpable buzz in the air.

The locals seemed lighter, more energized.

There was a strange, almost festive excitement everywhere she turned.

Curiosity growing, Emily turned to her Dutch boyfriend, Lars.

> "Hey, Lars, I've been hearing about something called *Rokjesdag*. What's it all about?"

Lars, a tall and confident Dutchman with a mischievous grin, let out a knowing chuckle.

> "Ah, *Rokjesdag*! It's the day when the sun finally graces us with its presence — and Dutch ladies start showing off their legs again in skirts and dresses."
>
> Emily's eyes sparkled with interest.
>
> "Sounds like a fun tradition! When does it happen?"
>
> Lars's grin widened. "Ah, my dear Emily, that's the tricky part. *Rokjesdag* is as unpredictable as Dutch weather itself. It might be April, May, even June. But don't worry — you'll know it when you see it."

Eager to witness it for herself, Emily kept a careful eye on the changing city.

Several weeks later, her patience was rewarded.

On a radiant morning, she awoke to a different kind of warmth in the air.

The sky blazed bright blue.

There was a lightness, a buzz, running through the streets.

Could this be it? she wondered, excitement rushing through her.

Stepping outside, Emily was greeted by a delightful surprise.

Everywhere she looked, Dutch women strutted confidently in skirts, dresses, and shorts of every color and style.

The city had transformed into a vibrant celebration of spring.

It was as if winter had been peeled away, replaced overnight by flowing fabrics and bright colors. Emily couldn't stop grinning.

Women of all ages walked with joy and pride, carefully chosen outfits fluttering in the breeze.

From floral patterns to bold solids, it was a feast for the eyes — and for the spirit.

In the midst of the colorful chaos, Emily spotted a familiar figure.

There was Lars, standing proudly in oversized sunglasses, trying (and failing) to look nonchalant.

Emily couldn't help but chuckle.

Gathering her best poker face, she strolled up to him and crossed her arms.

> "And just where do you think you're going, Mr. Mysterious?" she teased, a playful glint in her eyes.

Lars feigned innocence.

> "Oh, you know… just enjoying the beautiful day, soaking in the sun."
>
> Emily raised an eyebrow.
>
> "Interesting choice of eyewear, considering it's not that bright out."
>
> Lars shrugged casually.
>
> "Well, you know… gotta protect my eyes from the… uh, *Rokjesdag* glare."
>
> *"Uh-huh. Sure. You really think women don't notice the sudden explosion of male sunglasses on Rokjesdag?"*

Unable to hold it anymore, both burst into laughter.

Lars's playful facade crumbled completely.

"Okay, okay — you caught me. I thought I'd blend in. Guess the secret's out."

As they laughed together, Emily realized that *Rokjesdag* wasn't just about the weather.

It was about spirit — about celebrating lightness, shedding layers, welcoming a new season. And as Lars sheepishly removed his sunglasses, revealing twinkling eyes, Emily knew she'd remember this day. A perfect tale of springtime silliness — and, of course, a little ammunition for future teasing.

9

The Human Aquarium (A True Story)

Dutch lives on display - the most common thing for Dutch people

Walking in the streets of a Dutch village

Normally, I'd introduce a new character here, or revisit someone from earlier in the book, followed by a hypothetical — but all-too-likely — scenario they'd find themselves in.

But not this chapter, dear reader.

Instead of a fictional vignette, I'm sharing a true story — one that unfolded seven years ago, when I first brought my Portuguese partner, Alexandra, to the Netherlands.

It all began one brisk evening when we decided to take a stroll through the quaint Dutch neighborhood where I grew up: a rural area in the north, close to my parents' house.

It was supposed to be a casual walk — just a stretch of the legs and a whiff of fresh air.

Instead, it became a descent into the existential weirdness of Dutch transparency.

> "Why do they all live like this?" Alexandra asked, her voice tinged
> with disbelief, staring into yet another illuminated living room.

I followed her gaze.

There it was: a perfectly ordinary Dutch family in their natural habitat.

The father engrossed in a book, the mother sipping coffee while watching *Goede Tijden, Slechte Tijden*, the child gleefully playing on a tablet.

> "They do know we can see them, right?" Alexandra asked, squinting
> suspiciously.
>
> "Should we… I don't know… do something about it?"
>
> "What? Why? How?"
>
> My brain struggled to assemble coherent thoughts, let alone
> sentences.
>
> "Do what exactly? Close their curtains for them?"
>
> "Can you not see everything they're doing?" she insisted, gesturing
> toward the human diorama before us.
>
> "It's like a human aquarium!"

"Ah — you mean a *humarium*," I teased. (That was the wrong thing to say.)

Paranoia Sets In

By the next day, the discussion hadn't ended.

Or rather — from my native Dutch perspective — the paranoia had begun.

Alexandra became convinced that the Dutch weren't just casually displaying their lives; they were actively testing how others reacted to it.

Walking down the street became a high-stakes game of avoiding eye contact with every window.

"They're testing us," she muttered darkly one evening, narrowly dodging a lamppost.

"It's like they want us to see them, but the moment we do, it's somehow *our* fault."

Things escalated when she accidentally locked eyes with a man sitting by his fireplace, calmly eating a bowl of vla.

His expression shifted briefly from mild surprise to quiet confusion — clearly not recognizing her, yet somehow unsure whether he was supposed to.

Frozen like a deer in headlights, Alexandra did the only thing that felt natural:

She gave him a thumbs-up and bolted down the street.

"That man knows too much," she said grimly when I finally caught up.

Theories Gone Wild

As the days passed, Alexandra refused to let it go. (*To this day, she still hasn't.*)

Her curiosity spiraled into a series of increasingly absurd theories.

At first, she speculated it was tied to Dutch honesty — perhaps some kind of cultural bluff.

> "They have nothing to hide, so they show everything in their terrarium," she explained one evening, nodding sagely.
>
> "It's the opposite of Portugal, where you can't even tell if anyone's home."

But then, the theories took a turn.

> "What if it's a government thing?" she proposed.
>
> "Like… they're trained to live without curtains, so they won't hide anything from Big Brother? What if it's reverse surveillance?"

I couldn't help but laugh.

> "So you're saying the Dutch government teaches citizens to spy on themselves?"
>
> "Exactly," she said, dead serious.

Of course, I knew the real reason was far less dramatic — rooted in Calvinist traditions: honesty, modesty, nothing to hide.

But trying to explain that felt pointless.

She was too busy avoiding vla-guy's possible psychic surveillance.

A Cultural Role Reversal

We stayed in the Netherlands for a week.

Alexandra quickly realized it wasn't just a rural quirk:

Whether in a village or in a big city — the windows remained open, the living rooms remained illuminated, the lives remained visible.

By the end of the week, she reached a bizarre but oddly endearing conclusion:

"Maybe it's not that weird after all," she mused during another evening stroll.

"It's like they're saying: 'This is me. Look at my living room diorama. Take it or leave it.'"

She paused.

"Still, it's weird. That vla guy is probably waiting for me."

Hoping to distract her from creating more theories, I proposed a thought experiment:

"What if Dutch people moved to Portugal — and refused to use shutters or curtains?"

Her face lit up, instantly envisioning the chaos.

"They wouldn't last a day!" she declared.

"The neighbors would be at the window with binoculars, calling my *mãe* to gossip about the crazy foreigners showing off their IKEA furniture.

My uncle would probably show up with a hammer to fix their 'broken' shutters."

I laughed, picturing it.

"And what if the Dutch argued back? Said they were just being open and honest?"

"Open and honest?!" she scoffed.

"We don't do open and honest in Portugal. We do cozy and suspicious. It's part of the charm!"

(No Portuguese citizens were psychologically harmed in the making of this conclusion — though some Dutch living rooms may have been visually invaded.)

10

Birthday at the office

Apparently you can't have you cake or eat it.

Do you remember Dimitrios and Eleni?

Our Greek friends who had a slightly awkward dinner with their Dutch friends?

Well, today, instead of starting with explanations, we will follow the two of them during a birthday-filled month in The Netherlands.

At Work

As we know, Dimitrios lives in Groningen. However, he works as an administrator for a Dutch transportation company in the city of Leeuwarden, in the province of Friesland (Frisia).

In Dimitrios's third week, his colleague Pieter was congratulated by everyone — they sang a birthday song and even gifted him a small, awkward present: two stress relief dolls, one with the name of the office manager on it and the other with Pieter's wife's name.

It seemed like an insult to Dimitrios at first.

For a second, he was infused with angst at being an accomplice, having chipped in for the gifts.

But this faded quickly when he saw it was followed by thunderous laughter from everyone present — including the "insulted" parties themselves.

"Part of Dutch office banter, apparently," Dimitrios thought.

Moments later, Pieter went around the office with a box filled with treats.

When Pieter reached Dimitrios's desk, our Greek friend looked surprised at the contents and startled for a few seconds.

"Go ahead — that's oranjekoek, you'll like it," assured Pieter.

This clearly was not the birthday cake Dimitrios expected.

In fact, it was not a cake at all.

Dimitrios stared at a festive, square pastry: a sturdy base of rich buttery dough, enriched with cardamom and almond, covered in bright pink icing, topped with stabilized whipped cream, and finished with a piece of candied orange peel.

Because of the daunting appearance and inviting look, it was only seconds before the combined flavors met Dimitrios's mouth, tickling his taste buds and sending sugar-induced impulses straight to the pleasure cortex of his brain.

> "Hmmm... I love Dutch pastries," shared our relocating hero aloud
> — although he couldn't help but privately think,
> *"What in... [redacted for young readers] went wrong with Dutch*
> *cuisine?"*

"Congrats again! Doing anything fun today?"

"No, not really," Pieter replied.

"Since it's Friday, I'll celebrate during the weekend with a barbecue."

"Makes sense! Well, enjoy it! By the way, we're almost the same age — Monday I'll turn thirty-five like you did today," concluded our Greek friend.

"I knew it — you're a *broekje!* (*)" joked Pieter.

Dimitrios frowned.

"*Broekje?* I thought *broek* was pants... Wait, I'm small pants? What?"

Pieter laughed.

"*Broekje* means someone who knows nothing — just new to life. I guess 'rookie' or 'green' comes close in English.

Well — good weekend, *broekje!*" Pieter called, already halfway out the office.

(It was, after all, two minutes after closing hours.)

Dimitrios went home content, pleased with having experienced his first Dutch birthday at the office.

The gifts were odd, the pastries delicious.

> "Well, now I know how it's done. I'll fit right in next time."
> Or at least, that's what Dimitrios mistakenly thought...
> *(*)(Broekje: small pants/trousers — An inexperienced person who does*
> *not know much about life. English equivalent: "green" or "rookie.")*

Dimitrios's Birthday at the Office

Dimitrios headed into work Monday morning with a spring in his step, feeling confident he had cracked the code of Dutch office culture.

"What luck I had, experiencing that birthday last Friday. I know exactly what to expect now," sniggered our Greek friend to himself.

His internal fulfillment was betrayed by a wide grin — a grin that, for an outsider, might have been difficult to interpret.

And for a while, things went as expected:

A song he barely understood (except for the cheerful *"hoera, hoera!"* at the end).

Some awkward gifts.

An insistence that he open everything immediately.

His gifts included a desk flag — the Dutch national flag on one side, the Greek one on the other — some lovely stroopwafels, and, according to Dimitrios, some horrifying Dutch liquorice.

"Quite nice, thank you," he said — but it wasn't over yet.

Then came the card.

The card…

A nightmare for any HR department outside The Netherlands.

It bluntly stated that Dimitrios's work ethic was

"thankfully Dutch"

and…

"luckily not (yet) Greek — but only time will tell."

Dimitrios froze for half a second.

"Did they just call all Greeks lazy?!

While they themselves spend more time by the coffee machine than at their desks?! And work no more than 36 hours a week?"

These thoughts might have erupted in him, had he not already been seasoned by earlier experiences of Dutch blunt humor.

He remembered: this was a sign of acceptance — not hostility.

He mustered a laugh and fired back a light-hearted insult in return.

The room chuckled — and so he survived the ritual.

But it wasn't over yet.

"So, where's the birthday cake?" asked Ronald, the intern.

"Yes, where is it?" echoed Dimitrios playfully.

Silence...

Followed only by confused faces staring at him.

"Dude... don't tell me you forgot the cake?" Ronald said, half-laughing.

"But... it's *my* birthday..." stammered Dimitrios.

"**Exactly!**" came the chorus from his Dutch colleagues, all smiling like it was the most obvious thing in the world.

Dimitrios realized the cruel truth:...

In The Netherlands, you bring your own birthday cake!

"Darn you, Dutch culture! Stop throwing these curve balls at me!" Dimitrios screamed internally.

Apologizing profusely, he promised to bring something tomorrow — but sugar-craving colleagues weren't satisfied.

Jelmer, the department manager, took pity and extended Dimitrios's lunch break, personally giving him a lift to the local bakery.

That afternoon, our Greek birthday boy returned triumphantly... with *appeltaart*.

As he handed out slices, Dimitrios couldn't help but think:

"At this rate, I'll be singing Happy Birthday to myself by next year."

Another day, another file added to his internal *"Surviving Dutch Culture"* handbook.

"Well... surely a birthday at someone's home can't be that different, right?"

11

Birthday at someones home

Everyone is congratulated, why exclude the cats?

At a Dutch Birthday Party

It was a sunny Saturday for once, and Dimitrios, accompanied by his wife Eleni, embarked on yet another daring adventure — a grand Dutch birthday celebration.

Having learned from their previous encounters, they arrived just in the nick of time, only to discover that the party was already in full swing. Balloons adorned many corners, creating a lively, festive atmosphere.

As they approached the birthday girl, Rachelle, Dimitrios and Eleni enthusiastically congratulated her with three kisses each, thinking they had nailed the customary greeting.

Little did they know another hilarious mishap was lurking just around the corner.

Congratulating... Everyone?

Upon entering the party, they exchanged polite greetings with the other guests.

But soon they discovered that a simple "hello" and a smile weren't enough.

Just as they were taking a seat, their Dutch friends Nico and Maria strolled in, offering congratulations not only to Rachelle but also to David, her husband.

Eleni's eyes widened in confusion. Was it a double birthday she had somehow missed?

Before she could apologize for the oversight, Nico and Maria took it a step further.

They congratulated Rachelle's parents, her brother, and not one, but both her sisters.

It seemed as if the Dutch were on a mission to celebrate every single family member within reach.

> *"Dutch people must possess extraordinary powers to all be born on a single day!"*
>
> *Eleni thought to herself, barely suppressing a giggle.*
>
> *"Imagine the logistics of delivering all those babies within 24 hours!"*

Dimitrios exchanged a bewildered glance with Eleni.

Were they supposed to congratulate the entire nation next?

But after a quick mental calculation — perhaps aided by ancient Greek genes — they realized it was simply a quirk of Dutch culture: a tradition of congratulating everyone remotely related to the birthday person.

> *(This is true for many families and regions in The Netherlands, but not as widespread as other cultural aspects discussed in this book.)*

Amidst the joyful chaos, Dimitrios whispered to Eleni:

> *"I never thought I'd need a marathon training program just to keep up with birthday wishes!"*

Eleni stifled a laugh, envisioning a marathon runner leaping from family member to family member, barely catching their breath between congratulations.

And so, Dimitrios and Eleni dove headfirst into the whirlpool, congratulating distant cousins, second cousins, thrice-removed cousins, and anyone who dared to cross their path.

In fact, Dimitrios — growing more confident and perhaps a bit cocky — was the first to congratulate both family cats.

One cat ignored him entirely; the other walked off slowly, clearly annoyed when party guests followed Dimitrios's lead.

Birthday Gifts and Unwrapping

After what felt like congratulating half the town, it was time for the gifts.

Whilst Dimitrios might have picked up a hint from his office experience, he still wasn't prepared for the public unwrapping ritual.

He now regretted their choice of gift, but there was no stopping the Dutch anymore.

Rachelle began unwrapping each present one by one, delivering her honest verdict aloud after each.

The first gift, a cookbook for pasta, lasagna, and pizza, came from her aunt.

> "An Italian-food cookbook? You must have misunderstood — I love eating it, not cooking it!"

David chimed in, laughing:

> "Yeah, a cookbook won't help her for sure."

The witty aunt countered:

> "Oh, you both misunderstood. It's for David to read and use, so
> Rachelle can just enjoy the eating!"

Some gifts received genuine appreciation, but among the pile was a bright
poison-green T-shirt from her niece.
Rachelle's eyes widened. With a mischievous grin, she announced:

> "Oh, a bright poison-green T-shirt in my size! How nice! And how
> did you know I had nothing to wear yet for when I paint the house?
> It's perfect!"

The Greek Gift Disaster

But the real comedy gold was yet to come — unintentionally delivered by
Dimitrios and Eleni.
Nervously, they presented their gift: two bottles of wine.
One was a lovely dry red, and the other — carefully wrapped in bubble
wrap — had an attached note:

> *"A back-up in case you drop the first bottle again, like you regularly do
> on Friday evenings."*

Dimitrios froze.
This was definitely not the setting for the kind of banter they had learned
to survive at work.
He hadn't expected the gifts to be opened publicly in front of close family

members…— and now it was too late to retract their playful jab.

Rachelle blushed slightly, caught mid-laughter and mid-cringe, just as her grandmother piped up:

"Rachelle, my dear… you're not a drunkard, are you?"

The room hushed. Granny's narrowed eyes spoke volumes.

Eleni, quick on her feet, jumped in:

"Oh, no, no! It's a Greek thing! We love joking about things that aren't true. It's all in good fun!"

Granny remained skeptical, her raised eyebrow a testament to her lingering doubts — but Eleni's spirited defense was just enough to push the atmosphere back toward laughter.

The crisis was averted. Barely.

Later that evening, as they left the party hand-in-hand, Dimitrios sighed:

"Maybe next time… we just stick with a neutral plant?"

Eleni grinned:

"Or better yet… congratulatory treats for the cat."

Both burst into laughter as they disappeared into the soft Dutch night — once again, survivors of another round of cultural curveballs. For sure they got all Dutch birthday traditions down. *What could possibly still surprise them?*

12

Abraham & Sarah (turning 50)

An inflatable Abraham or Sarah & Musterd normaly sights when someone turns 50.

Abraham & Sarah

The sun shone brightly on another Saturday.

Dimitrios woke up, opened the shutters, and shockingly exclaimed:

"Eleni! Eleni! An air balloon landed in our neighbor's garden!"

When Eleni rushed to the window in disbelief, it became clear.

"That's not an hot-air balloon… that's a huge inflatable Abraham!"
She blinked at the sight.
"My dear, I knew the Dutch were tall, but that air-filled biblical figure is two stories high!"

They had been invited to the celebration across the road, celebrating the 50th birthday of their dear friend Peter — but this, clearly, was beyond anything they had expected.

Later, as they walked to the front door, Dimitrios turned to Eleni with a confident smile:

"You know, Eleni, after our last experience, I think we've mastered the art of Dutch birthdays. We've got this!"

Eleni chuckled, remembering the whirlwind of congratulations at their last party.

"Maybe we've learned a thing or two," she said playfully.
"But did you expect an Abraham who can look into our bedroom window? Let's not get too cocky — surprises seem standard here."

They rang the doorbell, and the door swung open to reveal a lively crowd inside.

Balloons and streamers decorated the house, but none as eye-catching as the towering Abraham grinning down from the garden, announcing Peter's entrance into the age of wisdom for the entire village to see.

Inside the Circle

Peter's wife, Annelies, greeted them warmly and ushered them into the living room — where guests had formed a perfect circle.

Dimitrios frowned slightly.

"What's this?"

"This is the *kring*," Annelies explained. "Let me grab two chairs for you."

Without needing to ask, the seated guests instinctively shuffled to expand the circle, barely interrupting their conversations.

Dimitrios and Eleni took their seats, feeling cautiously optimistic.

Dimitrios whispered with a grin:

"We've become Dutch birthday connoisseurs, haven't we, Eleni? Let's impress them!"

"What cake did Peter get for us?" Dimitrios asked Annelies, proudly showcasing his growing cultural knowledge.

"*Hazelnoot schuimtaart* — a light, hazelnut-flavored meringue cake. We'll serve it with coffee," Annelies replied warmly.

Meanwhile, Eleni rolled her eyes.

"You and your Dutch birthday expertise…" she muttered under her breath.

"Remember: we're always learning."

The Delicacies

As they settled in the *kring*, Dimitrios soaked in the atmosphere.

However, he quickly noticed something odd: no one mingled.

Some guests even ignored the person next to them, shouting across the circle to speak to someone several seats away.

Before Dimitrios could fully process the absurdity, Annelies arrived with a platter of traditional Dutch treats — cheese cubes (*kaasblokjes*) and bitterballen.

Dimitrios's eyes lit up.

"Ah, the delicacies of the Dutch! I can't wait to taste these!"

Eleni, however, recalled her previous run-ins with Dutch snacks.

Cautiously, she picked up a *kaasblokje* and took a bite.

Her eyes widened instantly, watering from the intensity.

"This cheese… it's the most intense cheese in the universe!" she gasped.

"It's like the taste of a thousand suns wrapped into one!"

The guests burst into laughter, appreciating her theatrical delivery.

"You didn't even add the spicy mustard!" one guest teased.

"She can't!" Peter added. "I'm the only one who knows where to get it!"

The mustard joke flew straight past Dimitrios and Eleni — but they laughed along anyway.

Feeling emboldened, Dimitrios helped himself to a bitterbal… and immediately regretted it. The scalding hot filling hit his mouth like molten lava, forcing him to spit it out reflexively.

"Oh, watch out! It can be hot," Peter said, clearly enjoying the escapades of his Mediterranean guests.

The Mustard Mystery

With the unconventional snacks savored (or survived), it was time for gifts.

The first gift Peter unwrapped was beautifully wrapped — almost intimidatingly so.

Dimitrios and Eleni exchanged worried glances.

> "Did we misunderstand again? Are lavish gifts expected for 50th birthdays?"

Their anxiety turned to confusion when Peter revealed the gift:
a cheap jar of mustard.

> "Ahh, but I don't need it anymore!" Peter laughed, holding it aloft.

Seeing their bewildered faces, Peter leaned over conspiratorially:

> "You see, when you turn 50, you're let in on the most sacred Dutch secret: the location where Abraham buys his mustard! I know now — but I can't share it with anyone who hasn't yet breathed 50 years of life."

Dimitrios and Eleni blinked.

Another mysterious Dutch ritual successfully added to their growing collection.

The Circle of Death

As the evening wore on, Dimitrios and Eleni had expected the party to loosen up.

But the *kring* remained… unmoving.

Static. Eternal.

Some expats have dubbed this phenomenon the *"circle of death"* — and now, our Greek couple understood why.

Returning from a bathroom break, Eleni noticed a seat free next to Annelies and innocently sat down.

"Oh, I'm sorry," Annelies said kindly. "That's Jasper's seat."

Confused, Eleni replied:

"Oh, no problem — I'll swap the chairs."

As Eleni bent down to swap the garden chair with her own, the room erupted in laughter.

Annelies quickly explained:

"No, no — it's *where Jasper was sitting.* Not the chair itself!"

Apparently, in the *circle of death*, your seat — once claimed — is spiritually bonded to you for the entire event.

"You can check out anytime you like... but you can never leave."

Eleni surrendered internally to the bizarre logic, while Dimitrios nearly cried from laughing.

The Walk Home

Later, walking back under the Dutch night sky, Dimitrios turned to Eleni, smiling:

"You were right. Dutch birthdays are full of surprises — but full of joy too.

The cheese, the mustard secret, the circle of death — unforget-table."

Eleni nodded, a mischievous smile tugging at her lips.

> "Absolutely, Dimitrios. But don't think I've forgotten — we still need
> to discuss you becoming far too Dutch."

They both laughed, their voices echoing down the quiet street — survivors
once again of another round of delightful Dutch madness.

13

Taboos in The Netherlands

Hidden taboos in The Netherlands

Taboos

At first glance, you might think Dutch people have no taboos at all.

After all, this is a country where topless sunbathing is normal, swearing during football matches is practically a second language, and friends might casually comment on your weight or haircut without thinking twice.

If you're used to a more cautious culture, it can feel almost liberating.

But spend enough time in the Netherlands, and you'll realize — **oh yes, there are taboos.**

They're just hidden in places you might not expect.

A Quick Peek at Dutch "Non-Taboos"

- **Nudity**? No big deal. At the beach, in the sauna, even in films — it's seen as natural, not automatically sexual.
- **Profanity**? Perfectly acceptable in the right context. Stub your toe, swear loudly — nobody will blink.
- **Comments on appearance**? Fair game. If your hair looks wild, a friend might cheerfully ask: "Ben je van de trap gevallen vandaag?" ("Did you fall down the stairs today?")

But when it comes to money — especially salaries — suddenly the famously direct Dutch turn strangely quiet.Talking openly about what you earn? Absolutely not done.

> *Although in more international workplaces, or among younger Dutch people, this taboo is slowly fading — but overall, discussing salaries still makes most Dutch people deeply uncomfortable.)*

Jack in Dokkum

Let's dive into a story to see how easily things can go wrong.

In the quaint town of Dokkum, there lived an American named Jack.

Recently relocated from bustling Boston, Jack was eager to immerse himself in Dutch culture.

One evening, he joined his new Dutch colleagues for after-work drinks at their favorite bar.

The atmosphere was buzzing with laughter and clinking glasses.

Jack, excited to bond, dove right into conversation.

After a few beers, his enthusiasm got the better of him.

> "So… how much do you guys make? The cost of living is pretty high here!"

A silence fell over the table.

Eyebrows raised.

The background chatter in the bar seemed to fade into stunned stillness.

(*If tumbleweed existed in the Netherlands, it surely would have rolled by.*)

Jack had — without even knowing it — walked straight into one of the country's few true taboos.

One colleague, Karel, eventually broke the tension with a grin:

> "Not enough! Right, everyone?"

Laughter erupted.

Jelle added:

> "Too little to live, too much to die!"

Marc finished:

> "As long as my boss pretends to pay me, I'll pretend to work!"

The crisis was averted, and Jack breathed a sigh of relief.

He thought he had learned the one critical rule.

Cultural Reversal: New Surprises

But the evening wasn't finished with him yet.

As the night wore on, the conversation turned far more personal — far more quickly than Jack was ready for.

Johnny casually mentioned his favorite sexual position.

Linda chimed in, asking a colleague which scenes from *Fifty Shades of Grey* they had tried.

Jack's eyes widened.

His participation dropped sharply as he tried to disappear into his beer.

In his American experience, conversations about sex were reserved for close friends — not casual colleagues at a bar.

When they eventually turned to him, asking for his opinion, Jack managed a weak smile and stammered through a vague, diplomatic response.

What parallel universe of social norms have I stumbled into? he wondered.

Despite the shocks and awkward moments, Jack realized something important:

Cultural differences were part of the adventure.

Sometimes hilarious, sometimes awkward — but always memorable.

When Jack eventually returned to the U.S. a few years later, he was full of fond memories:

Direct conversations, wild saunas, friendly bluntness… and a few unforgettable blunders.

Of course, when telling friends about his Dutch travels, he proudly listed Amsterdam, Antwerp, Brussels... and Copenhagen.

(Only one of those cities is actually Dutch — but that, dear reader, is a story for an American culture book.)

14

"The Dutch on Vacation: Masters of the Caravan"

Dutch on vacation bring their home and sometimes their own food. Hmm Dutch cuisine!

Holiday in Spain

Let's meet Henk and Ankje, a quintessential Dutch couple in their early fifties.

After months of planning, they've packed up their trusty caravan (nicknamed *De Hollander*) and hit the road.

Destination? Málaga — a sunny paradise promising "authentic Spain" with just the right amount of home comforts.

Sure, flying and booking an apartment might be quicker and cheaper —
but how else could they cook their trusty potatoes and have a place that
truly feels like home?

After a few days of driving, Henk pulls into their carefully selected
campground — researched for weeks on Zoover, of course.

They're delighted to find it's already half-Dutch.

Henk expertly maneuvers the caravan into a prime shady spot, while Ankje
sets up their folding chairs and orange-striped awning.

Within minutes, their corner of the campground looks like a tiny slice of
the Netherlands:

a hanging Dutch flag, potted plants from home, and their beloved Senseo
coffee machine plugged into the caravan.

"Cultural Immersion," Dutch-Style

Their first evening in Málaga is carefully planned.

They stroll hand-in-hand to the beachfront terrace of a restaurant with a
laminated menu offering paella, pizza, and schnitzel.

> "Look, Ankje, they even have bitterballen!" Henk exclaims, pointing
> at the *Dutch Snacks* section.

At exactly 18:00 — prime Dutch dinner time — they settle in, puzzled by the
lack of locals around them.

> "These Spaniards must be pulling overtime," Ankje chuckles.

Over dinner, Henk adjusts his wraparound sunglasses — futuristic shades he
is convinced make him look sporty.

Ankje nods approvingly, though the locals probably think he looks like a
cycling coach lost at sea.

They sip their sangria (with ice cubes — how fancy!) and admire the
souvenir stalls selling flamenco dresses and plastic castanets.

"This is clearly the real Spain, sun and all," Ankje marvels.

The Art of the Discount

The next day, Henk and Ankje explore the promenade, drawn to a stall selling "handmade" leather handbags.

A smiling vendor greets them enthusiastically:

"Only €200! The finest leather in Málaga!"

For Henk, it's game on.

"No way, that's robbery!" he declares in Dutch, nudging Ankje with
a conspiratorial wink.

After fifteen minutes of dramatic haggling — complete with sighs, head shakes, and dramatic walkaways —

Henk triumphantly secures a "steep" discount.

At €100, he beams proudly as the vendor thanks him profusely.

"See? That's how you handle these vendors!" Henk boasts in Dutch.
"They can't fool me."

Nearby, a vendor mutters to his colleague in Spanish:

"Another Dutchman — always thinks he's winning."

Reluctance to Splurge

Later at the beach, Henk balks at paying €12 for a sun lounger rental.

"€12 for a chair? Outrageous!"

Instead, they drag their trusty folding chairs to the sand — plunking down in front of a group of British teenagers blasting reggaeton from a Bluetooth speaker.

> "Why do they have to be so loud?" Ankje grumbles, scrolling through her phone.

Meanwhile, Henk dutifully lathers on SPF 50 — keeping his white socks firmly on under his sandals.

> "Just in case we go for a walk later," he mutters.

As the sun sets, they return to the campground.
Over coffee with their Dutch neighbors, Henk can't resist bragging:

> "We found this incredible leather stall! Got a bag for half price — only €100.
> The vendor practically gave it away!"
> "And the sangria!" Ankje adds. "Not too sweet. Very authentic."

Their neighbors nod politely, clearly hearing the same story for the third time today.
Henk, not finished, pulls out his phone to show his mileage app.

> "You won't believe this — we've driven 2,235 kilometers so far!
> Only filled up twice! These Germans know how to make an engine, don't they?"

An "Authentic" Farewell
By the end of their week-long holiday, Henk and Ankje are bursting with pride over their "immersive" Spanish experience.
They've explored the local mall, stocked up on imported Gouda at Carrefour,
and even joined a group excursion to an olive oil factory (which included

free samples).

As they hitch up the caravan and head home, Henk pats the dashboard.

"What a great trip," he says.
"We've really soaked in the Spanish culture."

Meanwhile, back at the promenade, vendors toast to another successful tourist season.

"To the Dutch lobsters!" one laughs.
"Long may they haggle — and think they win."

15

Lost in Translation

A monkey and something comes out of his sleeve?

Game-Night

The doorbell rang exactly at 8 p.m., and Mike and Anna exchanged a glance.

Punctuality wasn't something they were used to — but Willem and Marijke, their Dutch neighbors, were nothing if not prompt.

The bell rang again, this time with Willem's cheerful voice:

"We know you're home! It's almost one minute past eight! We are here!"

Mike sighed.

"Guess there's no playing it cool in the Netherlands."

When they opened the door, Willem and Marijke stood beaming, a Tupperware container in hand.

"We brought bitterballen!" Marijke announced brightly.
"Oh, thanks!" Anna said, not entirely sure what bitterballen were.
"Come in! We're just setting up the games for tonight."
"Ah, you're running Dutch time minus five minutes. Very efficient!" Willem grinned.
"Very good. We are ready to win the games."
"Uh… it's just for fun," Mike added carefully.
Willem arched an eyebrow.
"Sure. Fun. I am not falling for that."

Game 1: Dutch-English Scrabble
They started with Scrabble, allowing a mix of Dutch and English words —
which, naturally, led to chaos.
Marijke confidently placed *huisarts* on the board.

"Sorry, what's that?" Anna asked.
"House doctor," Willem said. "You call it… general practitioner?"

Mike frowned.

"I'm not sure that's allowed. It has to be one word."
"It *is* one word," Willem insisted, looking personally offended.

Anna decided not to argue and played *lending*.
Willem peered at the board skeptically.

"What is *lending*?"

"When you temporarily give money to someone and get it back later," Anna explained.

"No, that is *loaning*," Willem said with the confidence of a man completely wrong.

"Loaning is what the borrower does. Lending is what the lender does," Mike clarified.

Marijke nodded, laughing.

"In Dutch, we just call both *lenen*. That's why Willem is confused."

The game continued — and Willem smugly played an enormous word: *fietsbandventieldopjesdoos*.

Anna squinted.

"Is that… real?"

"Of course! It means the box where you keep the caps for bike tire valves. Very useful."

Mike groaned.

"I feel like the Dutch are just trolling us now."

Game 2: Pictionary

Next was Pictionary.

Willem grabbed the marker and quickly drew what looked suspiciously like… a monkey trapped inside a sweater.

"A monkey?" Anna guessed.

"Yes! But not just a monkey," Willem said, adding an arrow to a sleeve.

"What is the monkey doing?"

"Crawling out of a sleeve?" Mike ventured.

"Exactly! The monkey comes out of the sleeve! It means the truth is revealed."

Anna stared.

"Why was the monkey in a sleeve in the first place?"
Marijke shrugged.
"It's surprising, isn't it? Where else would a monkey be?"
"Anywhere *but* a sleeve!" Mike said, throwing his hands up.

Their turn. Anna drew a stick figure under an umbrella with cats and dogs falling from the sky.

"Is it about pets? A zoo?" Marijke tilted her head.
"No, it means it's raining really hard," Anna laughed.
Willem frowned.
"Why would cats and dogs fall from the sky when it rains? That makes no sense."
"Honestly?" Mike admitted. "We have no idea either."

Game 3: Charades

Last was charades.
Willem leapt up, miming eating, then crossed his arms in frustration.

"Dinner?" Mike guessed.
"Food?" Anna tried.
"No!" Willem said, exasperated.
"It's the saying! *Ik heb er geen kaas van gegeten!*"
"Something about cheese again? Why is it always cheese?" Anna groaned.
"It means 'I know nothing about it,'" Willem explained proudly.
"You can't know a cheese until you eat it. If you know nothing about something, you say this."

Mike gaped in silent amazement.

"Your cats and dogs saying makes zero sense," Willem shot back.

"At least ours are well thought through."

Bitterballen and Lingering Confusion

After the games, Willem triumphantly retrieved the Tupperware.

"Here, fry these. Bitterballen. Very Dutch."

"What's in them?" Mike hesitated.

"Meat… sauce… something," Willem shrugged.

"Just eat it. You'll like them."

Anna popped one in her mouth and nodded approvingly.

"Okay, these are good! Like croquettes."

"No!" Marijke said, scandalized.

"They are *not* croquettes!"

"Of course not," Mike muttered.

As the night wore on (and the drinks flowed), linguistic disasters continued. After Willem spilled his drink on Marijke, he exclaimed:

"Now we make that good later!"

"You mean… clean it up?" Mike blinked.

"It can bother me nothing!" Marijke chimed in cheerfully.

"You mean 'I don't care?'" Anna frowned.

Finally, Willem stood up, satisfied.

"This was fun! We won 3–0! Haha! Better luck next time. Next time, we teach you Sinterklaas traditions!"

"Like what?" Mike asked suspiciously.

"Zwarte Piet! And *pakjesavond!"* Willem announced with glee.

Mike and Anna exchanged a wary look.

"Sure," Anna said slowly.
"Sounds… educational."

As the door closed behind their guests, Mike collapsed onto the couch.

"At least we survived."
"Barely," Anna agreed.
"But hey, we learned two important things tonight."
"Yeah? Like what?"
"First: never trust a monkey in a sleeve.
Second: Dutch people either don't hold back… or our neighbors are completely insane."
As she cleaned up, Anna spotted a lone bitterbal hiding under the couch.
"Great. Now we'll have bitterballen ghosts haunting us until we finally become fully Dutch.

16

Sinterklaas - Pakjesavond

December 5th, aka 'pakjesavond'

Pakjesavond Panic

Klaas and Linda had done it again: a cozy living room filled with snacks, *kruidnoten*, candles, and just enough tension to feel like December in the Netherlands.

Their house looked like it had been lightly sneezed on by a *pepernoten*-scented fog machine.

This time, they'd invited everyone — Dutch friends and expats alike — to experience a "proper" Sinterklaas evening.

There would be singing.

There would be gifts.

There would be poems.

There would be confusion.

Naturally.

Invited were Willem & Marijke (their Dutch neighbours), Pablo & Isabella (our Spanish couple), Mike & Anna (USA), and Dimitrios & Eleni (our Greek couple).

Warming Up (and Immediately Derailing)

The evening began with Marijke passing out printed song sheets — complete with all 14 verses of *Zie Ginds Komt de Stoomboot* and a few lesser-known hits that seemed to have been photocopied from a 1983 church songbook.

Mike and Anna, armed with cautious optimism, began reading the lyrics aloud.

> *"Zie ginds komt de stoomboot uit Spanje weer aan,*
> *Hij brengt ons Sint Nicolaas, ik zie hem al staan..."*

Mike paused.

"Wait. He comes from Spain?"

Anna nodded.

"Apparently. With presents. And cinnamon cookies."

"Why would he leave Spain by boat for the Netherlands in winter?"

Meanwhile, Willem was singing with operatic flourish.

Eleni clapped politely.

Dimitrios joined in enthusiastically, replacing half the words with Greek syllables.

Pablo hummed.

Isabella just smiled — the smile of someone who didn't know what was happening, but had decided to enjoy it anyway.

That was when Mike — between verses — whispered:

"Didn't *we* invent this? Santa Claus? Coca-Cola? Red suit? American ad guy?"

"Nope," Klaas said flatly.

"Dutch. Saint Nicholas. 4th century. Bishop. Turkey. The whole thing."

Anna added, "Actually, it was a Dutch copywriter at Coca-Cola. *You* copied *us*."

Mike made a note.

'Accidentally American imperialism. Again. Next they'll tell me that apple pie is also from Holland.'

What Even Is Sinterklaas?

As songbooks were tucked away, snacks passed around, and gifts placed in a large heap by the fireplace, the conversation took a turn.

"So let me get this straight," said Mike, holding up a *kruidnoot* like it might contain answers.

"This holiday involves:
- A Catholic clergyman in red robes,
- Blackface assistants who sneak around at night,
- Children sitting on a stranger's lap who pretends to be a Catholic clergyman."

He paused.

"Did I get that right?"

Linda's smile tightened.

"Well... if you say it like *that*..."
"You're missing the point!" Klaas added, panicking slightly.
"But most surprisingly of all, if you're bad... you get taken to sunny Spain?"

Isabella, already halfway through a mug of *glühwein*, chimed in cheerfully:

"I think it's brilliant. If I'm good, I get a dry cinnamon cookie.
But if I'm naughty, I get transported to a warm country with good

wine and beaches?"

"I think you want people to be naughty. The only thing missing is some kind of whip that you can spank the 'naughty' person with."

Willem started to respond.

"Well actually we had the *roe*… which—"

"Sssst," said Marijke. "They have a bad enough impression as is…"

"*Now* I am convinced," Pablo nodded. "I think it's secretly a strategy to convince Dutch women to be naughtier."

Marijke took a sip of tea and replied without blinking:

"We call that *liberated.*"

Laughter from the foreigners. The Dutch people don't understand why.

Gift Time (and the Coaster Incident)

"Time for gifts!" Linda declared.

Everyone clapped — except one person.

Dimitrios.

He was staring in horror at the wrapped present he'd brought, slowly realizing something was missing.

Not the gift.

Not the wrapping.

Not the Sinterklaas spirit.

The poem.

"Dimitrios?" Eleni asked sweetly. "Did you forget the rhyme?"

His face paled.

Everyone turned.

"Well," Klaas said, rubbing his hands. "Guess we know who your assigned person is!"

With the whole room watching, Dimitrios grabbed a green Heineken coaster, flipped it over, and began scribbling furiously with a red pen Linda had thrown to him like a life preserver.

"Dear Mike,
You are very tall.
Sint did not forget you at all.
This gift is to eat.
Best regards from a controversial Piet."
There!"

He held it up. The room applauded like the man had just defused a bomb using only chewing gum.

The Surprise That Just. Would. Not. End.
Next came Pablo and Isabella's turn.
They unwrapped a gift addressed *"Para Los Reyes de Orange."*
It was a box.
Inside the box… another box.
And inside that… another one.

"Is this a prank? Or a Russian doll box?" Pablo asked.
"No," said Willem. "It's a surprise."
"Surprise that I now hate wrapping paper," muttered Isabella.

Finally, they reached the core — a small, orange tea towel.

"Is this festive or existential?"

The Creepy Surprise

Anna opened her gift next.

Inside: a huge chocolate letter *L* and a poem that began ominously:

"You turn off lights, but not the loo,
    The hallway's bright, the bulb is new.
    And every night when Mike is still watching TV, your neighbours can hear you hum,
    And before he comes to bed you have already c.—"
"*That's* enough! Thank you — very nice," said Mike.
"Who wrote this?" Anna asked, raising an eyebrow.
Willem raised his hand . 'I guess a Piet did it, they see everything you know' zero shame

"Well it is quite accurate, Anna joked, and scary to know.. but the chocolate letter does certainly help."
    "I'm buying blackout curtains for my soul," concluded Mike.

The Final Rhyme (Domestic Edition)

Finally, Klaas opened his gift from Linda.

Inside: a jar of mustard and a handmade mug that read *"I survived December."*

His poem read:

"Dear Klaas, A dear. A stoic man,
    Who leaves his socks in every pan.
    You sing too loud. You talk too much.
    You sneeze with drama, and then you clutch
    Your chest like opera, for effect.
    But Linda still chooses you. (Mostly. With regret.)"

Klaas smiled.

"This is romantic," he said.

Linda nodded, sipping tea.

"It's also a warning."

As wrapping paper and empty wine cups piled up, Klaas raised his glass.

"To Sinterklaas and Z… and Piet!"
"To Sinterklaas! And surviving poetry from expats!" Marijke added.

Dimitrios sighed with relief. Pablo raised the orange tea towel in silent salute. Mike whispered to Anna:

"Next year, I bring a lawyer."

And tucked between the cushions, a lone *kruidnoot* waited patiently for next year's victims.

17

A Dutch newsarticle: How to Politely Kick Out Your Guests After Christmas Dinner

Ah, the great Dutch paradox:

You've spent hours perfecting your *kerstdiner*, served up *gezelligheid* in heaping portions, and now… the guests simply won't leave.

Your couch is pleading for liberation, the dishes are mounting like a Delft Blue avalanche, and your *gezelligheid* reserves are teetering dangerously low.

What's a host to do?

Enter Jan Jaap van Weering, Dutch etiquette aficionado and savior of overstretched hosts everywhere.

In an interview for NU.nl with Carolijn Melters, Van Weering offers the ultimate advice for overstaying guests — delivered with quintessential Dutch practicality.

His first tip? **Manage expectations before the first round of bitterballen even hits the table.** Casually mention an end time right at the beginning:

"We'll wind things down around ten."

Which, in Dutch cultural code, translates to:

"You'll be on your way by eleven at the latest — or else."

If subtle hints fail and Uncle Kees looks ready to launch into a multi-hour holiday anecdote marathon, it's time to escalate.

Use **tactful directness, Dutch style**:

- Yawn dramatically.
- Stand up and start clearing the table at record speed.
- Channel your inner Marie Kondo — preferably the Dutch Edition.
- Bonus move: say something like, *"I'll handle the cleaning after you leave!*

This delicate balance of honesty and warmth is peak Dutch culture.

They've somehow mastered the art of saying *"Please leave now"* without causing offense — or at least without compromising *gezelligheid*.

It's a form of social jujitsu that many expats find both shocking and deeply enviable.

For those of us who hail from cultures where the evening ends only when the host passes out face-first in a plate of leftovers, this approach feels revolutionary.

It's not just about reclaiming your sofa;

it's about maintaining a relationship without post-dinner passive aggression.

After all, there's nothing less *gezellig* than inviting guests you secretly resent because they stayed until the milkman arrived.

So this Christmas, channel your inner Jan Jaap.

Let your guests know when *gezelligheid* has reached its natural conclusion.

With any luck, they'll even thank you for sparing them the agony of wondering: "Is it too soon to leave?" Because nothing says "Happy Holidays" quite like Dutch honesty — wrapped neatly in a bow of politeness.

This piece was inspired by **the NU.nl article: Hoe je gasten na het kerstdiner beleefd je huis uit krijgt by Carolijn Melters.**

18

BONUS Chapter: Fairytale TickTockville: Anti-Social Behaviour in Middle-Aged Holland

TICKTOCKVILLE
TIME IS EVERYTHING!

Before we close this book, I wanted to leave you with a little gift: a bonus story.

It's written in a different style — a fairy-tale twist on Dutch punctuality.

Enjoy this final and now fully fantasy-adventure through the land of clocks, confusion, and a very mischievous boy.

A Fairy-Tale

Once upon a medieval time in the land of rain, windmills, wooden shoes, and stubborn people there was a small village called Ticktockville, known for its obsession with punctuality. The villagers, mostly Dutch, took their timekeeping very seriously. They had the most accurate clocks in the world, even **Big Jan**, the famous town clock was synchronized down to the second. The village was truly Dutch as everyone ate bread for lunch and even the local cats scheduled their hunting time.

Joa the Trickster

One day, a mischievous young boy named Joa, *of Portuguese origin* (who was clearly jealous of the punctuality and efficiency of the village) decided to play a prank on the villagers. He thought it was time for some light-hearted fun, and was curious to see what would happen if the trusted schedules would be impacted.

So, he hatched a plan to confuse the entire village and **prove** the supremacy of leading a relaxed and wine-filled life.

He convinced the local clockmaker, **Mister Altijd van der Time**, that it would be really cool if he would help him pull off a small little innocent prank.

Late at night, Joa sneaked into the small village square and climbed up the old clock tower. He carefully adjusted the clock, turning the hour hand forward by one hour.

As a result, the next morning, everyone woke up thinking they were already an hour behind.

Chaos

Panic ensued as the villagers rushed to their workplaces, schools, and appointments. The milkman arrived at people's doorsteps while they were still fast asleep. The baker's bread was ready before sunrise.

This all could,… theoretically,.. still be forgiven.

But even the mayor was impacted — he arrived at the town hall to deliver a speech to an empty room.

Which he still delivered — because it was on schedule, after all.

Even the local roosters became confused to the extent that they thought the sun had risen late that day.

Confusion reigned. Utterly.

The villagers scrambled for answers. Some marched to neighboring villages to ask if they too were experiencing a time anomaly.

News spread like wildfire, and soon the whole region was buzzing with stories of the time-traveling town.

Joa's Victory (Sort Of)

Meanwhile, Joa watched the chaos unfold from his hiding spot. He couldn't help but laugh at the sight of everyone's puzzled faces.

But his mischief didn't go unnoticed for long.

The village clockmaker — now full of regret — realized what was going on and that he should never have helped Joa.

Mr. Van der Time, armed with his trusty pocket watch (and possibly a very firm frown), embarked on a mission to restore order to Ticktockville.

He carefully adjusted each clock back to its original time, ensuring that every second was accounted for.

The Return to Normal

Slowly but surely, the village returned to normal.

People started arriving at their appointments on time.

The rhythm of daily life resumed.

The prank was never forgotten — and neither was Joa: the first troll in recorded history who thought he was cool, but in reality, all he did was discomfort the honest, hard-working people in town whilst making a fool of himself.

He never realized that while laughter is a wonderful thing, it's essential to find the right balance between mischief and respect for the routines and habits that make a community tick and tock.

The Legacy

And so, Ticktockville continued its proud tradition of timekeeping — albeit with a little more caution, knowing that even the most punctual of places can experience a time hiccup now and then.

In fact, in honour of Ticktockville. or perhaps in honour of Joa many years later, an app was developed.

> A digital place where people can proudly share their **dumbest, most anti-social behaviour**, thinking they're cool, funny, and adored.
> The truth?
> I guess Joa went on to have many children who all think they are cool doing silly dances blocking escalators.

About the author

About the Author

Steven van Holland has spent the last fifteen years doing something incredibly Dutch: explaining the Netherlands to people who didn't ask — and usually ended up grateful anyway.

A trained communication expert and seasoned Dutch teacher, Steven has taught both locals how to talk to each other *zonder gedoe*, and internationals how to survive awkward birthday circles, licorice trauma, and the national obsession with "just being honest."

When not untangling Dutch culture to the intrigued, he roams the world with a laptop and a strong opinion about punctuality. He's lived, worked, and accidentally offended people from the USA to Portugal, and from Poland to the UK — collecting both cultural insights and confused looks.

> *Lekker Direct* is his very Dutch attempt at making sense of a culture that makes no sense at all — unless you grew up in it. And even then, it can still be a bit confusing.